# Rosie's New Harness

BY CHARLIE TENNESSEN
ILLUSTRATED BY CHLOÉ WRIGHT

A TEAM ANARCHY STORY

## Rosie's New Harness

Rosie was concerned. Her harness had been missing for days. The Friendly Farmer took Cassie and Sebastian to plow the field without her! What happened to her harness? Was she still part of the team? The first book in the Team Anarchy series brings readers into the life of the donkeys and their experiences with (and without!) a complete team on their animal-powered farm.

## Artist's Note

The illustrations in this book are original watercolor paintings on acid-free cold press paper.

**anarchy acres**

A Team Anarchy Story

Text copyright © 2017 by Charlie Tennessen
Illustrations copyright © 2017 by Chloé Wright
All rights reserved.

ISBN: 978-1-7322558-1-4
LCCN: 2018904873

Book design by Allison Thielen.

## Coming Soon: Popcorn Day

The day Cassie saved the popcorn harvest on Anarchy Acres!

anarchyacres.com/books

For Rosie.
You came, and then
we were a team.
-Charlie

For Charlotte,
Neil and Quinn.
My very own team
of determined little
donkeys.
-Chloé

Rosie was concerned.

Three days earlier, right after morning chores, the Friendly Farmer had removed her harness from the rack in the barn and taken it into the shed. The harness, which normally hung on the wall of the barn next to the other harnesses, was gone.

Each morning Rosie would check the hooks where her harness was supposed to hang, and it was still missing. "What's he doing with my harness?" said Rosie. "Did he sell it? Am I off the team?" She was very worried.

"What if I have to pull something?"

"Oh, Rosie,"
said Sebastian.

Sebastian rarely
said anything else.

Rosie, Cassie, and Sebastian
are three small donkeys,
with big hearts,
who live together on a tiny
farm in Wisconsin.

The farm is known as Anarchy Acres, and the three donkeys are known as Team Anarchy.

Cassie, the spotted donkey,
said nothing but kept her eye on the shed.
For three days, the Friendly Farmer had been
spending his spare time in the shed.
Noise and dust came out of the shed
when he was in there.

Nobody knew what was happening inside the shed.

Donkeys need a harness so they can pull things. Rosie, Cassie, and Sebastian loved to pull things for the Friendly Farmer. Even though they were small donkeys, when they worked together, they could pull all sorts of things. If Team Anarchy did not work together, even if each donkey had a harness on, they could not pull much of anything.

The next day, the Friendly Farmer came out to the barn and put harnesses onto Cassie and Sebastian.

They were hitched to the plow
and together they went down to plow
the lower field, leaving Rosie alone
in the corral. Alone!

Donkeys do not like to be left alone.
A donkey by itself does not feel safe,
and will try hard to join
the other donkeys.

Rosie was unhappy in the corral and could only pace and watch as Cassie and Sebastian plowed the field without her.

Rosie could not know it, but the Friendly Farmer was anxious to get the lower field plowed. There was rain in the forecast, and wet fields cannot be plowed.

Since Rosie's harness was not hanging on the hook in the barn, she could not be hitched with the team. Cassie and Sebastian had to pull much harder without her help.

Cassie and Sebastian came back to the barn after an exhausting morning in the field. They were both very tired. "Rosie! It's so much harder without you," said Cassie. "I wish you had been there to help today."

"I wanted to help, too," said Rosie.
"I just need to have my harness.
**WHERE IS MY HARNESS?**"
Rosie was more concerned than ever by now.

Later that week the Friendly Farmer came out of the shed, carrying something strange.

Cassie snorted when she saw him walk towards the corral.

Donkeys don't see very well and can get confused or scared if something doesn't look right.

The Friendly Farmer put the strange object down on the fence. It was a new harness, a harness that he had just finished making in the shed!

It had a wide, strong collar with blue padding.
The straps looked strong and all the hardware was shiny.

Rosie and the other donkeys cautiously walked over to see what was hanging from the fence rail.

Rosie sniffed at it, and she sensed something familiar.

There were parts from her old harness,

but also some new parts!

Could THIS be her harness?

Soon Cassie and Sebastian joined Rosie in examining the harness hanging on the fence.

Donkeys do not experience the world in the same way that people do, so the team was not exactly sure what they were sniffing at. But they were curious about the harness, and they knew it was something familiar.

The Friendly Farmer picked up the new harness and said, "Whoa," to Rosie. Rosie stood still while the harness was draped over her neck and body.

Gradually she realized, this was her **NEW HARNESS!**

The collar felt very comfortable around her shoulders and neck. The back straps and the belly band were just the right length. The blue padding near her shoulders looked beautiful. Rosie was very happy.

"I LOVE MY NEW HARNESS!" she cried out.

"Let's go pull something... NOW!"

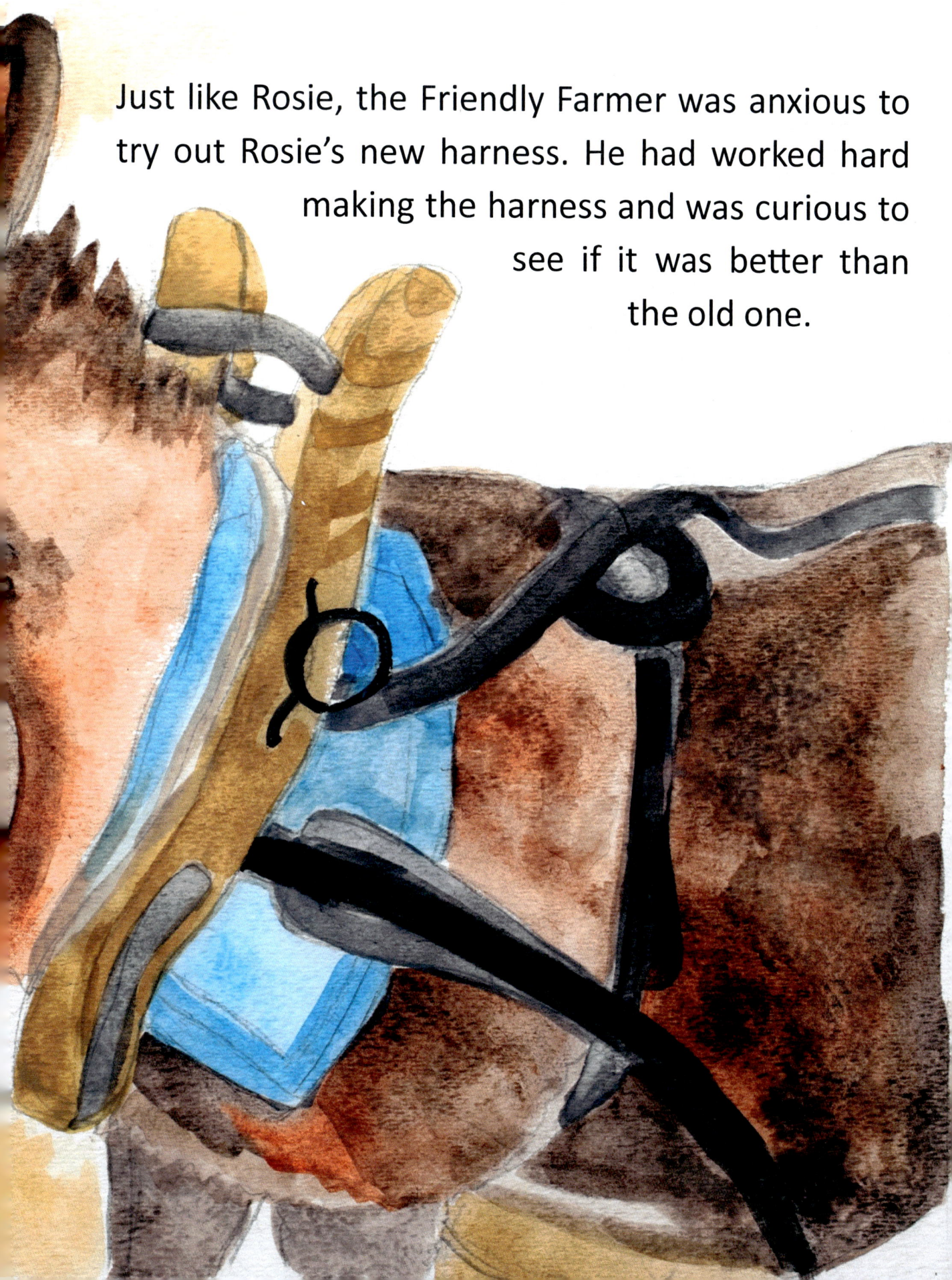

Just like Rosie, the Friendly Farmer was anxious to try out Rosie's new harness. He had worked hard making the harness and was curious to see if it was better than the old one.

Cassie and Sebastian stood still while their harnesses were strapped in place.

Each donkey had a bridle put on, and the lines were attached to the bits. Rosie was hitched up on the left side, Cassie in the middle, and Sebastian on the right.

All three donkeys would be pulling together today!

To test out the harness, the Friendly Farmer hooked up Team Anarchy to the work sled. Rosie felt her shoulders pushing into the blue padding of her collar. The new harness felt wonderful!

"Look at me everyone! I can pull so hard now, and it doesn't hurt!"

# "I LOVE MY NEW HARNESS!"

Together,
the four of them,
Rosie, Cassie, Sebastian, and the Friendly Farmer,
spent an enjoyable afternoon moving compost with the
work sled. The donkeys were happy to be working again.
And they were very happy to have Rosie back on the team.

Rosie would not stop talking about her new harness.

# "I LOVE MY NEW HARNESS!"

she said, over and over.

"Oh, Rosie,"

Sebastian replied.

This was about the most that Sebastian ever said.

# About the Author

Wisconsin native Charlie Tennessen discovered donkey-powered farming by accident as a second act to his previous life as a web developer.

# About the Illustrator

Chloe Wright is an artist, illustrator, mom and yoga instructor based in Racine, Wisconsin.